What's in this book

This book belongs to

_____

你见过它吗?
Have you ever seen it?

学习内容 Contents

沟通 Communication

描述动物外貌

Describe animals

背景介绍：
自然界中的动物千姿百态，而神话故事中的神奇鸟兽，往往是人们根据现实生活中的动物加以想象而创造出来的。

生词 New words

★	它	it
★	鱼	fish
★	鸟	bird
★	有	to have
★	没有	not to have
★	长	long
★	大	big
	身体	body
	翅膀	wing

虎鲸

秃鹰

鲸鲨

驼鸟

句式 Sentence patterns

它有翅膀。

It has wings.

它有长长的身体。

It has a long body.

它没有耳朵。

It does not have ears.

文化 Cultures

中西文化中的凤凰

The phoenix in Chinese and Western cultures

跨学科学习 Project

认识动物的行动方式

Learn about how animals move

Get ready

世界上最大的鱼是鲸鲨，而最大的动物是蓝鲸。蓝鲸属于鲸目，虽然人们通常把鲸叫做"鲸鱼"，

1 What is the biggest fish in the world? 但它们其实是哺乳类动物。

2 What is the biggest bird in the world?

3 What is the strangest animal in your mind?

tā

它

我们用"它"来指代人
以外的单个事物。

niǎo

鸟

yú

鱼

故事大意：
传说中，有一种动物是鱼也是鸟。当它是鱼时叫鲲，
它的身体有几千里长。它可以变为鹏鸟，振翅一飞
可以飞上半天高。

它是鱼，也是鸟。

参考问题和答案：

1　Do you think this creature looks strange? (Yes, it looks very strange.)
2　What does it look like? (It looks like the combination of a fish and a bird.)

cháng

长

它有长长的身体。

参考问题和答案：
1 What can you see in the picture? (I can see the body of the creature.)
2 Is the body long or short? (It is very long.)

dà
大

它有大大的翅膀。

参考问题和答案：

1   What can you see in the picture? (I can see the creature's wing.)
2   Is the wing big or small? (It is very big.)

你见过它吗？

参考问题和答案：

1 Do you think the creature can fly? (Yes, it has big wings.)
2 Do you think it can swim too? (Yes, it has the body of a fish.)
3 Have you seen this creature before? If you have, where have you seen it?
   (Yes, I have. I have seen it in a Chinese storybook./No, I have not.)

没有人见过它，因为……

"没有"和"有"是一对反义词。

参考问题和答案：

No one has ever seen the creature in real life. Do you know why?
(Because it is not real./Because it has a secret hiding place.)

它生活在神话里。

参考问题和答案：

1　What can you see in the book? (The creature.)
2　What do you think the book is about? (It is about mythical creatures.)
3　Do you like the story about this creature? (Yes, it is very interesting./No, I like real animals only.)

延伸活动：

问问学生有哪些生物在现实生活中是不存在的。可以列举例子供学生讨论，如：中国龙（Chinese dragon）、凤凰（phoenix）和独角兽（unicorn）都不存在、恐龙（dinosaur）曾经存在、鸭嘴兽（platypus）存在。

Let's think

1 Look at the pictures and think. Put a tick or a cross.

这是鸟。 ✗

这是鸟。 ✓

这是鱼。 ✗

这是鱼。 ✓

2 Draw your favourite animal and talk about it.

学生可用 "它是……" "它有/没有……" 等句式描述。

New words

1 Learn the new words.

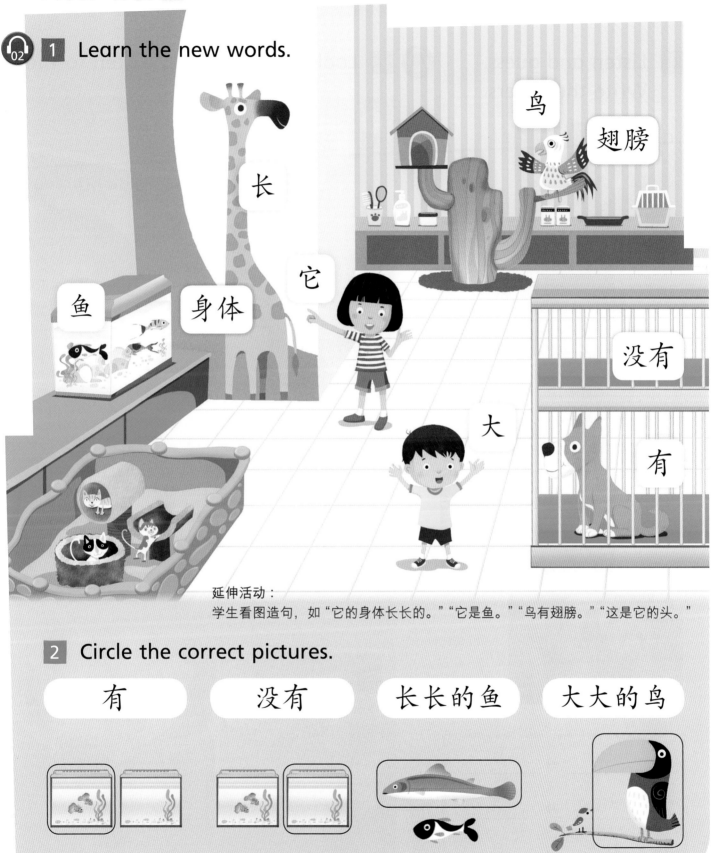

长

它

鱼

身体

鸟

翅膀

没有

有

大

延伸活动：
学生看图造句，如"它的身体长长的。""它是鱼。""鸟有翅膀。""这是它的头。"

2 Circle the correct pictures.

| 有 | 没有 | 长长的鱼 | 大大的鸟 |

听听说说 Listen and say

 1 Listen and guess.
Write the letters.

 2 Look at the pictures. Listen to the sto

① 这是什么？

② 它有大大的嘴巴和身体。

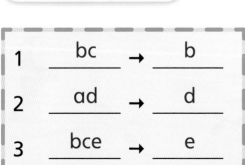

1	bc	→	b	
2	ad	→	d	
3	bce	→	e	

学生根据每题录音的前半句，先罗列出所有符合条件的动物，再根据录音后半句，筛选出正确答案。

nd say.

3 Listen to your teacher and guess. Write the letters.

它有大大的耳朵和身体，
它有长长的鼻子，
它喜欢吃香蕉，
它是什么？ | b |

鸭嘴兽是生活在澳大利亚的哺乳动物。它的长相很有趣，看起来像是几种动物的混合体。其嘴巴和脚蹼像鸭子，尾巴像海狸，身体和皮毛像水獭。

这是鸭嘴兽，platypus。
你见过它吗？

猴子 | a

大象 | b

恐龙 | c

猫 | d

它有没有翅膀？

它没有翅膀。

它没有翅膀，
它喜欢玩，
它喜欢吃鱼，
它是什么？ | d |

它有长长的身体，
它没有翅膀，
没有人见过它，
它是什么？ | c |

13

Task

提醒学生尽量运用已学的词、句来描述动物。

Show a photo of your favourite animal and introduce it to your friends.

我喜欢熊猫 (panda)。
它有大大的身体。
它没有翅膀。

Paste your photo here.

Game

学生两人一组，在数数过程中互相监听，检查对方能否正确数出图中鱼和鸟的数目。

Count in Chinese to check if the numbers of fish and birds in the pictures are correct.

29

正确

21

正确

Song

学唱歌前先问问学生是否知道图中的都是什么鱼和什么鸟。

 Listen and sing.

锦鲤（koi），一种观赏鱼，原产于中国。

秃鹰（bald eagle）是美国国鸟。

它是鱼，

它是长长的鱼。

它是鸟，

它是大大的鸟。

长长的鱼，你见过吗？

大大的鸟，你见过吗？

派克鱼（pike），一种淡水鱼。

鸵鸟（ostrich），生活在非洲，是世界上最大的鸟类，但不会飞。

孔雀（peacock），雄鸟的尾毛展开像扇子，不会飞。

课堂用语 Classroom language

翻开书本第8页。
Turn to page 8.

打开书包。
Open the school bag.

 写一写 Write

1 Learn and trace the stroke. 老师示范笔画动作，学生跟着做：用手在空中画出"横撇"。

横撇 フ フ フ フ

2 Learn the component. Circle 鱼 in the characters.

学生观察图片，引导他们发现"鱼"字的意思。

3 The writing of 鱼 has changed over time. Look at the characters and colour the fish. 引导学生从左至右观察"鱼"字写法的变化。告诉学生，"鱼"字从最开始的像图画一样的写法逐渐变得越来越适合书写。

延伸活动：
学生发挥想象，自创"鱼"字的新写法。完成后，老师收集全班学生的作品，贴在班级展示区展示。

4 Trace and write the character.

汉字小常识 Did you know?

Can you match the pictures to the scripts? Write the letters.

a 羊 　　 b 马 　　 c 鸟 　　 d 虎 　　 e 牛

c 　　 e 　　 a 　　 b 　　 d

第二、第三个象形字比较相像，对应"牛"和"羊"，提醒学生注意羊角和牛角的方向以区分。第四、第五个象形字也比较容易混淆，对应"马"和"虎"，提醒学生根据两个动物的最显著特征来配对文字，如：马背上有鬃毛，而老虎有爪子。

多元学习 Connections

Cultures

凤凰是中国古代传说中的百鸟之王。雄的叫"凤"，雌的叫"凰"，但后来其形象慢慢被看作阴性。古代常用龙作为帝王的象征，而凤凰则是皇后妃嫔的象征。而在西方文化中，凤凰被视为"不死鸟"。一种说法是当它到达五百岁时，它会用香木筑巢自焚，再从灰烬中重生。

1 The phoenix is an ancient mythical creature in both the East and the West. Have you ever seen one?

In China, phoenix is an important symbol of peace, nobility and beauty.

In the West, phoenix is associated with the sun and rebirth, symbolizing renewal.

2 Colour the phoenix and talk about it.

它有大大的翅膀。

它……

参考答案：它有大大的翅膀。它有长长的身体。

1 Group the animals by how they move. Write the numbers.

Fly	Swim	Walk
2 5 7	4 6 11 12	1 3 8 9 10 11

1 斑马
2 鹌鹑
3 狮子
4 鲸
5 秃鹫
6 八爪鱼
7 小鸟
8 熊猫
9 浣熊
10 长颈鹿
11 海狮：既可以在水里游泳，又可以在陆地上爬行。
12 X光鱼

2 Can you find any animal which can both fly and swim? Show and describe it.

学生可以拿一张动物的照片或将动物画出来，再进行介绍。

它的……

它有……

它是……

参考动物：
天鹅、海鸥、部分鸭子

温习 Checkpoint

1 Answer the questions from Sphinx to get into the pyramid.

游戏方法：
学生两人一组，一人扮演斯芬克斯，一人扮演浩浩，从金字塔底部依照线路提示依次回答问题/书写汉字。回答完最后一题，浩浩便可成功进入金字塔。

埃及金字塔是古埃及法老的陵墓，其中最大的是胡夫金字塔。在胡夫金字塔的附近有座狮身人面像，是按神话中人面狮身的斯芬克斯为原型建造的。在神话故事中，斯芬克斯总是拦住路人让他们猜谜。

Can you write the character 'fish'?

它喜欢吃什么？
它喜欢吃鱼。

它有没有翅膀？
它有翅膀。

Can you say 'It has a big mouth' in Chinese?
它有大大的嘴巴。

Can you say 'It has a big body' in Chinese?
它有大大的身体。

你见过我吗？
我没有见过你。

它是什么？
它是鸟。

你几岁？
我六/七/八岁。

我叫 Sphinx。你叫什么名字？
我叫……

20

2 Work with your friend. Colour the stars and the chillies.

Words and sentences	说	读	写
它	☆	☆	🌶
鱼	☆	☆	☆
鸟	☆	☆	🌶
有	☆	☆	🌶
没有	☆	☆	🌶
长	☆	☆	🌶
大	☆	☆	🌶
身体	☆	🌶	🌶
翅膀	☆	🌶	🌶
它有翅膀。	☆	🌶	🌶
它有长长的身体。	☆	🌶	🌶
它没有耳朵。	☆	🌶	🌶

Describe animals	☆

3 What does your teacher say?

分享 Sharing

延伸活动：
1 学生用手遮盖英文，读中文单词，并思考单词意思；
2 学生用手遮盖中文单词，看着英文说出对应的中文单词；
3 学生两人一组，尽量运用中文单词复述第 4 至第 9 页内容。

Words I remember

它	tā	it
鱼	yú	fish
鸟	niǎo	bird
有	yǒu	to have
没有	méi yǒu	not to have
长	cháng	long
大	dà	big
身体	shēn tǐ	body
翅膀	chì bǎng	wing

Other words

也	yě	also, too
人	rén	people, person
见过	jiàn guo	to have seen
吗	ma	(question word)
因为	yīn wèi	because
生活	shēng huó	to live
在	zài	at, in
神话	shén huà	myth
里	lǐ	inside
鸭嘴兽	yā zuǐ shòu	platypus
熊猫	xióng māo	panda

OXFORD
UNIVERSITY PRESS

Oxford University Press is a department of the University of Oxford.
It furthers the University's objective of excellence in research, scholarship,
and education by publishing worldwide. Oxford is a registered trade mark of
Oxford University Press in the UK and in certain other countries

Published in Hong Kong by
Oxford University Press (China) Limited
39th Floor, One Kowloon, 1 Wang Yuen Street, Kowloon Bay,
Hong Kong

© Oxford University Press (China) Limited 2017

Illustrated by Anne Lee, KK Ng, KY Chan and Wildman

Photographs for reproduction permitted by Dreamstime.com

China National Publications Import & Export (Group) Corporation is an authorized distributor of
Oxford Elementary Chinese.

Please contact content@cnpiec.com.cn or 86-10-65856782

ISBN: 978-0-19-082143-2

10 9 8 7 6 5 4 3 2

Teacher's Edition
ISBN: 978-0-19-082155-5

10 9 8 7 6 5 4 3 2